Poggy
and the Flies

Written by Joy Cowley
Illustrated by Anne Sulzer

Poggy Frog sat by the pond, eating green flies.

Zzzzz! Zzzzz!

Slurp!

Lizzy Lizard sat by the pond, eating blue flies.

Zzzzz! Zzzzz!

Crunch!

Poggy Frog said to Lizzy Lizard,
"I like green flies."

Lizzy Lizard said to Poggy Frog,
"I like blue flies."

4

"Green flies are best!"
said Poggy Frog.

"Blue flies are best!"
said Lizzy Lizard.

"Green flies! Green flies!"
shouted Poggy Frog.

"Blue flies! Blue flies!"
shouted Lizzy Lizard.

Then they stopped talking.
Poggy Frog sat by the pond,
eating green flies.
Zzzzz! Zzzzz!
Slurp!

Lizzy Lizard sat by the pond,
eating blue flies.

Zzzzz! Zzzzz!

Crunch!

Along came Hissy Snake.
"What are you eating?"
asked Hissy Snake.

"Green flies!" shouted Poggy Frog.
"Green flies are best!"

"Blue flies!" shouted Lizzy Lizard.
"Blue flies are best!"

Hissy Snake smiled.

"Green flies are not best.

Blue flies are not best.

Frog and lizard are best."

"Frog and lizard? Oh no!"
thought Poggy Frog.
Away he went, splash, splash,
into the pond.

"Frog and lizard?
Oh no!" thought
Lizzy Lizard.
Away she went,
run, run, up a tree.

Hissy Snake laughed
and laughed.

Then Hissy Snake sat by the pond,
eating green and blue flies.
Zzzzz! Zzzzz! Slurp, crunch!
Zzzzz! Zzzzz! Slurp, crunch!